DATE DUE

AP 21 '95		
MY 28 '97		
OC 20 '97		
DE 3 '00		

The '70s

Life in a Dumb Decade

by Jim Ryan

HARMONY BOOKS / NEW YORK

Published by Harmony Books, a division of Crown Publishers, Inc., 201 East 50th Street, New York, New York 10022. Member of the Crown Publishing Group.

HARMONY and colophon are trademarks of Crown Publishers, Inc.

Manufactured in the United States of America

Library of Congress Cataloging-in-Publication Data

Ryan, Jim, 1960–
    The '70s : life in a dumb decade / by Jim Ryan.—1st ed.
        p.   cm.
    1. American wit and humor.   2. Wit and humor, Pictorial.   3. United States—Popular culture—Humor.   4. United States—Social conditions—Humor.   I. Title.
PN6162.R93   1992
741.5'973—dc20   91-43665
                                                                                  CIP

ISBN 0-517-57221-4

10 9 8 7 6 5 4 3 2 1

First Edition

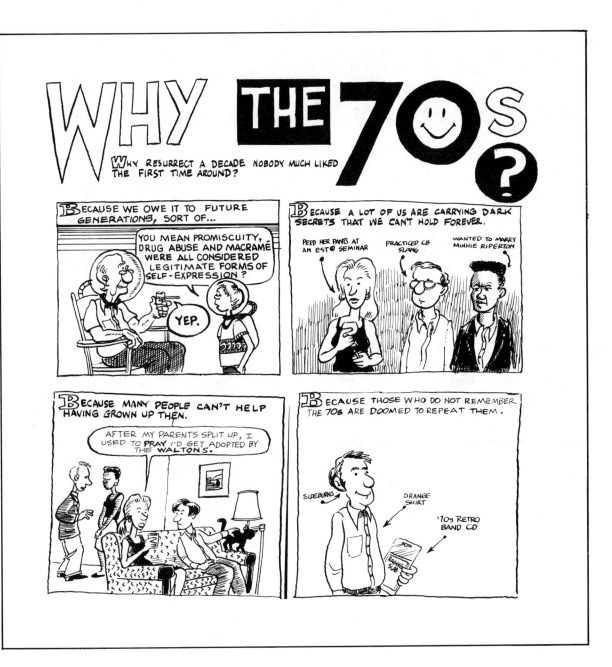

WHATEVER HAPPENED TO...

"HAPPYFACE:"
UNABLE TO COPE WITH HIS FAME,
'70s FOLK HERO "HAPPYFACE" BECOMES
A RECLUSIVE ALCOHOLIC AND DIES
IN 1981 FROM COMPLICATIONS OF LIVER JAUNDICE.

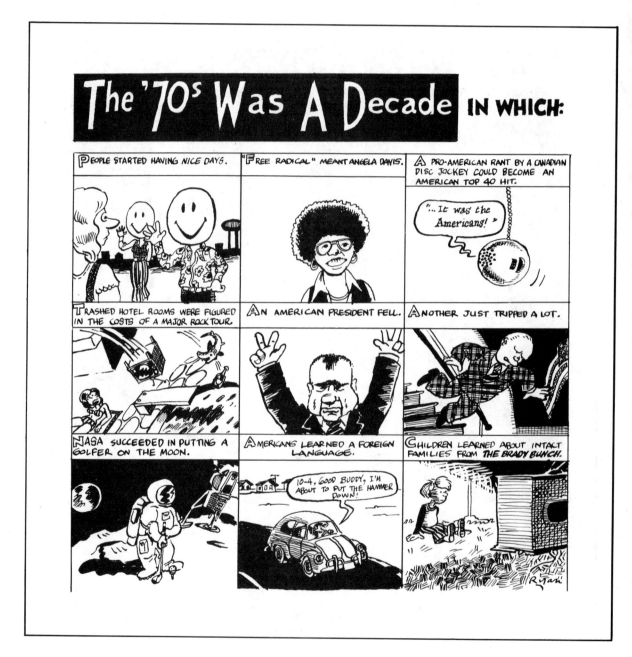

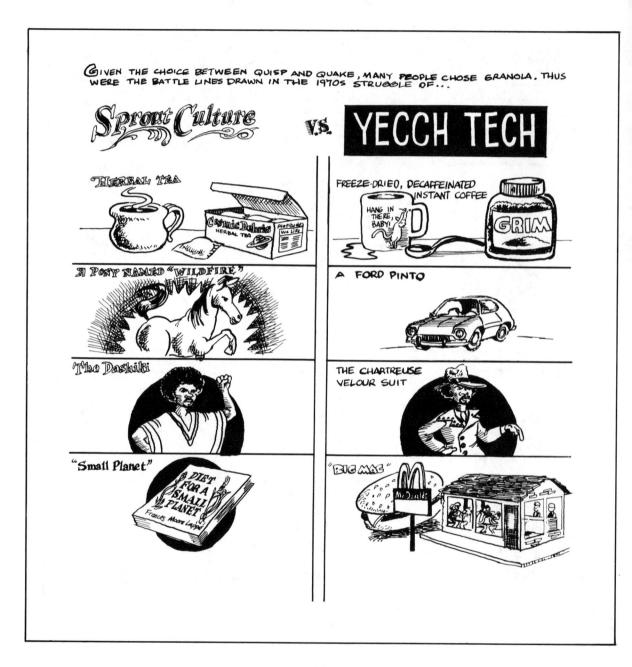

GIVEN THE CHOICE BETWEEN QUISP AND QUAKE, MANY PEOPLE CHOSE GRANOLA. THUS WERE THE BATTLE LINES DRAWN IN THE 1970s STRUGGLE OF...

Sprout Culture VS. YECCH TECH

HERBAL TEA

Cosmic Debris HERBAL TEA

FREEZE-DRIED, DECAFFEINATED INSTANT COFFEE

HANG IN THERE, BABY!

GRIM

A PONY NAMED "WILDFIRE"

A FORD PINTO

The Dashiki

THE CHARTREUSE VELOUR SUIT

"Small Planet"

DIET FOR A SMALL PLANET
Frances Moore Lappé

"BIG MAC"

McDonald's

Hippie Nostalgia

"The Modern World is not so bad, not like those students say."
—Jonathan Richman

Clunky, Old Fashioned Lettering à la R. Crumb

COMMUNES WHERE HIPPIES LIVED THE PASTORAL IDYLL OF HARD WORK, COMMUNAL LIVING AND INADEQUATE SANITARY FACILITIES

AN OUTBREAK OF DULCIMER MUSIC

SEPIA-TONED ALBUM COVERS THAT COULD HAVE BEEN TAKEN BY MATHEW B. BRADY

Ferd's Farm

LARD-RENDERING AND GEEGAW-MAKING EXPLAINED FOR YOUNG MODERNS

Foxfire

EXPENSIVE LOOMS TO BE UNLOADED CHEAP AT 1981 GARAGE SALES (BY PEOPLE WHO'D LEARNED WHY THE INDUSTRIAL REVOLUTION WAS A GOOD IDEA)

THE "PEASANT LOOK": WORN BY PEOPLE WHOSE ANCESTORS LEFT EUROPE FLEEING THIS PARTICULAR FASHION STATEMENT

17

Airbrush Van Culture

Remember the construction workers who used to beat up peace marchers? The yokels who blew away Dennis Hopper in *Easy Rider?* Well, by 1974, substantial numbers of their children were smoking pot, swapping mates and customizing airbrush vans. Airbrush van culture was hippy hedonism minus political leftism grafted onto the roadhouse and kustom kar culture of working class America. While former '60s radicals were pondering their betrayed ideals in Cambridge and Berkeley, kids from Southie and Oakland were digging Led Zep on the van's eight track, rollin' doobies, screwing chicks and having the time of their lives untroubled by ideological angst.

Remembering *Casual Sex*

CASUAL SEX WAS GREAT, EXCEPT WHEN IT WASN'T, WHICH WAS A *LOT* OF THE TIME, OR WHEN EVEN THE PERMISSIVE MORES OF THE DECADE WOULDN'T MAKE IT HAPPEN, WHICH WAS *MORE* OF THE TIME. BUT SOMETIMES IT *WOULD* HAPPEN, AND THEN IT WOULD BE GREAT — OR AWFUL, DEPENDING.

BEAM ME UP, SCOTTY.

Casual Sex WAS MADE POSSIBLE BY A GRANT FROM THE PLAYBOY FOUNDATION ... AND BY THE FOLLOWING CONDITIONS:

#1 IF YOU TOOK PRECAUTIONS, CHANCES ARE YOU WOULDN'T GET PREGNANT.

#2 WHAT YOU COULD GET WAS GENERALLY CURABLE WITH...

A DOSE OF ANTIBIOTICS

Krab Away — A TOPICAL OINTMENT

ABOUT 15 SHOWERS

UGH! YECCH! GROSS!

SEXUAL *REVOLUTION* HIGHLIGHTS

1970

1971

1972 FIRST ORAL SEX IN IOWA

1973 THE PRESIDENT OF THE SMALL MIDWESTERN COLLEGE ASSOCIATION HITS ON A SURE-FIRE ENROLLMENT BOOSTER.

Dear Penthouse Forum,

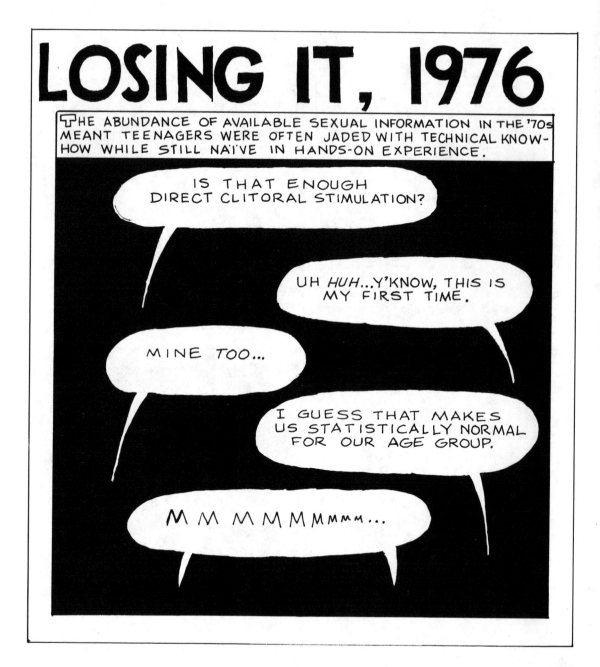

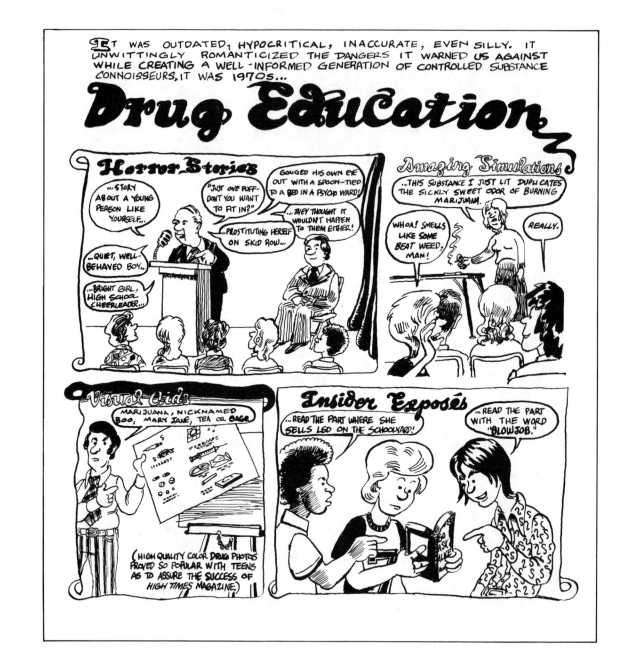

"I AM" MUSIC ...AND I WRITE THE SONGS!"

Seventies radio hits were divided between the stupidly profound and the profoundly stupid. The worst ones conveyed a wizened, metaphysical world weariness as only a stoned twenty-year-old can manage. A few bars of "DUST IN THE WIND" could send an optimists'club chairman running to the gas oven. Songwriting talents that once would have been overtaxed rhyming "moon" and "June" felt compelled to pen album-length meditations on existential anomie. Meanwhile, a crop of novelty hits arose, any one of which made "PURPLE PEOPLE EATER" sound like a Bach cantata. (Chuck Berry's only #1 hit was "MY DING-A-LING" in 1972.) This mating of the solemn and silly produced some bizarre offspring.

At Last! YOU Can Have The Last Word

In *All* Your Don McLean-related Arguments!

Now you can **always have** a definitive interpretation of the 1971 generational classic *Right* at your fingertips!

- Twenty years in the making!

- Compiled, written and edited by the world's *top* McLean scholars!

- Approved by the prestigious Lost Sixties' Ideals Research Institute of Berkeley, California!

- Each volume's binding individually handstitched by beautiful hippie girls in flowing Indian print dresses!

Just a sample of the insights you'll gain...

McLean's Verse:

Well, for ten years[1] we've been on our own
And moss[2] grows fat on a rolling stone[3]
but that's not how it used to be[4]

When the jester[5] sang for the King[6] and queen[7]
In a coat he borrowed from James Dean[8]
and a voice that came from you and me

Our Interpretation:

1. Ten Years: McLean wrote his classic in 1970 - ten soul-searching years after the New York City bus drivers' strike of 1960.

2. Moss: a veiled reference to Moss Hart, beloved dramatist of the American musical stage

3. A reference to Roland Stone, drama critic to whom Moss Hart owed much of his reputation in Cincinnati

4. McLean seems to be saying that's not how it used to be.

5. Harold Stassen, whose repeated bids for the Republican presidential nomination made him a figure of fun.

6. Dwight Eisenhower, elder statesman of the Republican party

7. Mamie Eisenhower

8. Reference unknown. Possibly McLean meant Jimmy Dean, country music star and eventual sausage magnate.

MUSICIAN ATTRITION

JAMES M. HENDRIX 1942-1970

YEAR	ARTIST	DEATH OR BREAKUP	REASON	EFFECT
1971	JIM MORRISON		FOUND DEAD IN THE BATHTUB OF HIS PARIS APARTMENT... POSSIBLE OVERDOSE OF DRUGS and/or MR. BUBBLE.	GAVE ROCK WORLD ANOTHER DEAD SEX SYMBOL. GAVE IGGY POP A STAGE ROUTINE. GAVE CRYSTAL SHIP A CAREER. GAVE THE CITY OF PARIS CAUSE TO REGRET BURYING HIM.
1970	The BEATLES		"ARTISTIC DIFFERENCES" AND THE PROSPECT OF PLAYING THE INDIANA STATE FAIR IN 1981	LEFT THE FIELD OF PRETENTIOUS "CONCEPT" ALBUMS & "SYMPHONIC" COMPOSITIONS TO BE PICKED CLEAN BY OTHER BANDS. GAVE DIEHARDS A REUNION TO ANTICIPATE UNTIL DECEMBER 1980.
1970	Jimi Hendrix		DRUG OVERDOSE, PASSED OUT AND CHOKED ON HIS OWN VOMIT.	INSPIRED MANY MUSICIANS TO PLAY FEEDBACK-LACED GUITAR SOLOS. INSPIRED OTHERS TO OVERDOSE, PASS OUT, AND CHOKE ON THEIR OWN VOMIT.
1970	JANIS JOPLIN		HEROIN OVERDOSE	PROVIDED ANOTHER ROLE MODEL FOR SELF-DESTRUCTIVE FEMALE BLUES SINGERS. FILLED OUT THE "J'S" IN THE "GOOD DIE YOUNG" ALPHABET.
1971, 72, 74, ETC...	CROSBY, STILLS, NASH & YOUNG		FORMED, BROKE UP, RE-FORMED, BROKE UP AGAIN, THROUGHOUT THE DECADE	GAVE NEIL YOUNG A LOT OF SOLO CAREERS

More MUSICIAN ATTRITION

YEAR	ARTIST	DEATH OR BREAKUP	CAUSE	EFFECT
1971	DUANE ALLMAN		MOTORCYCLE CRASH	DUANE WAS MERCIFULLY SPARED SEEING HIS BROTHER GREGG WITH CHER ON THE COVER OF _ALLMAN AND WOMAN_.
1973	JIM CROCE		PLANE CRASH	GREAT CAREER MOVE
1974	"MAMA" CASS ELIOT		HEART ATTACK (RUMORED TO HAVE CHOKED ON A HAM SANDWICH.)	SHOCK, GRIEF, SICK JOKES
1978	KEITH MOON		THREE GUESSES	• **WHO ARE YOU** GOT SOME MUCH-NEEDED CHART MOMENTUM • NO MORE DROWNED ROLLS-ROYCES
1979	SID VICIOUS		ONE GUESS	IMPROVED HIS BASS PLAYING

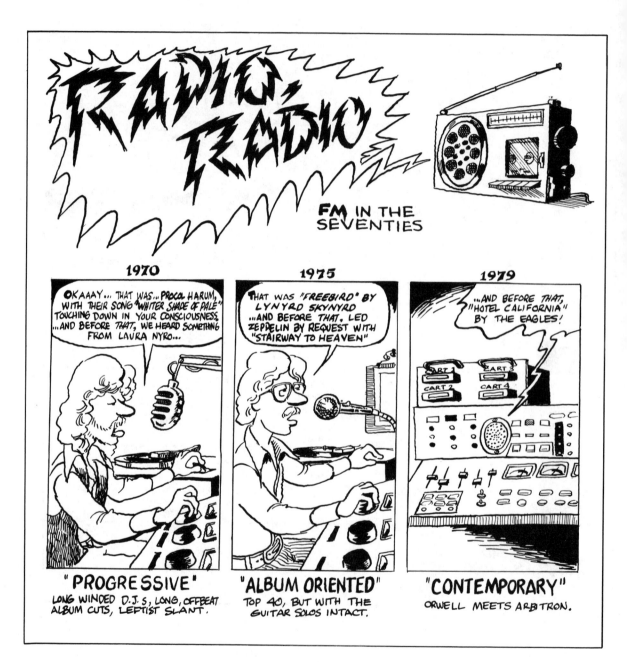

Disco Mementos:

Gold Chains
(Great for accessorizing chest hair)

UNH UNH UNH UNH STAYIN' ALIVE!

Instructional book and soundtrack to *Saturday Night Fever* for home study.

White *John Travolta* suit with indelible sweat stains

CIRCA 1977 INSTITUTIONAL-SIZED CANS OF POPULAR DRINK MIXES

HOLIDAY HOUSE® Brand PIÑA COLADA MIX

HOLIDAY HOUSE® Brand TEQUILA SUNRISE MIX

HOLIDAY HOUSE WHITE RUSSIAN MIX

EMPTY COKE VIAL

HALF A 'LUDE

BROKEN AMYL NITRATE "POPPER"

HERPES SIMPLEX

"EVERYBODY WAS KUNG FU FIGHTING"

"Them cats was fast as lightning
In fact it was a little bit frightening
But they fought with expert timing"
—CARL DOUGLAS

KUNG FU MOVIES CAPITALIZED ON THE ETERNAL YEARNING OF 98-POUND WEAKLINGS TO WHALE ON BIG BULLIES.

GO!!

HI-YAH!!

IN THE EARLY '70s THIS YEARNING WAS PERSONIFIED IN BRUCE LEE, ACTOR AND KUNG FU INNOVATOR. HE WAS A POWERFUL, SEXY CHINESE MAN WHO WAS NEITHER MAO ZEDONG NOR HOP SING.

UGH.

BRUCE LEE NOT ONLY DID WONDERS FOR THE HONG KONG FILM AND TRAMPOLINE INDUSTRIES, HE LEGITIMIZED WHAT AMERICANS CALLED "DIRTY FIGHTING" SIMPLY BY BEING A MORE APPEALING ORIENTAL MARTIAL ARTIST THAN HAD EVER BEEN ON THE AMERICAN SCREEN.

PRE-BRUCE LEE CONCEPTION OF KARATE GUY

...WHICH INSPIRED NOT ONLY 98-POUND WEAKLINGS BUT ALSO THE BIG BULLIES WHO WERE IN A POSITION TO DO SOMETHING ABOUT IT.

I GOT A THIRD DEGREE BLACK BELT IN KARATE.

...BUT I NEVER USE IT UNLESS SOMEBODY LOOKS LIKE THEY'RE GONNA LOOK AT ME FUNNY.

46

The Kohoutek Syndrome

KOHOUTEK WAS A COMET WHICH, ACCORDING TO ADVANCE HYPE, WAS GOING TO MAKE HALLEY'S LOOK LIKE A FLASHLIGHT BULB. SOMEHOW, IT DIDN'T SHOW UP AS PROMISED, THUS QUALIFYING AS THE GODOT OF ASTRONOMICAL PHENOMENA. THE DECADE WAS FILLED WITH THESE KINDS OF NON-STARTERS

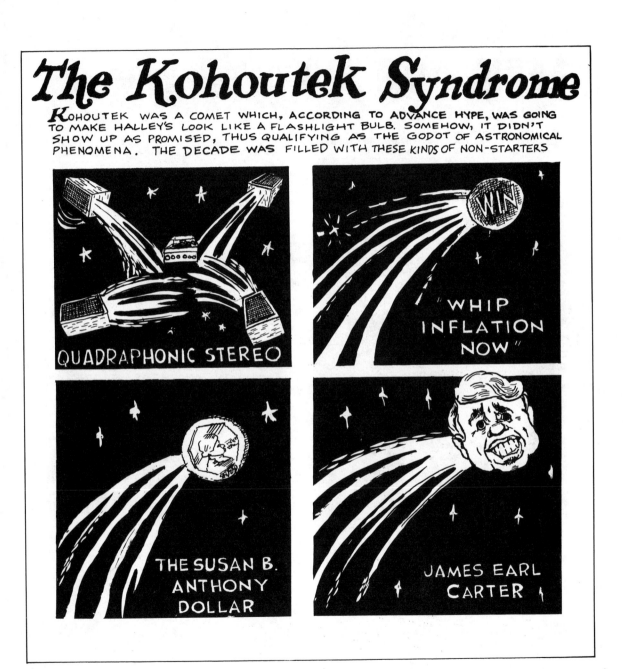

QUADRAPHONIC STEREO

WHIP INFLATION NOW

THE SUSAN B. ANTHONY DOLLAR

JAMES EARL CARTER

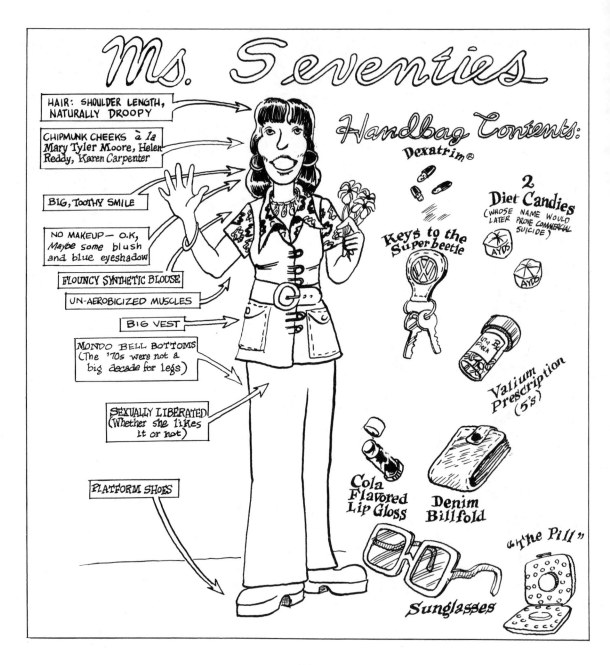

Ms. Seventies

HAIR: SHOULDER LENGTH, NATURALLY DROOPY

CHIPMUNK CHEEKS à la Mary Tyler Moore, Helen Reddy, Karen Carpenter

BIG, TOOTHY SMILE

NO MAKEUP — O.K, *Maybe* some blush and blue eyeshadow

FLOUNCY SYNTHETIC BLOUSE

UN-AEROBICIZED MUSCLES

BIG VEST

MONDO BELL BOTTOMS (The '70s were not a big decade for legs)

SEXUALLY LIBERATED (Whether she likes it or not)

PLATFORM SHOES

Handbag Contents:

Dexatrim ®

2 Diet Candies (WHOSE NAME WOULD LATER PROVE COMMERCIAL SUICIDE)

AYDS AYDS

Keys to the Super beetle

Valium Prescription (5's)

Cola Flavored Lip Gloss

Denim Billfold

"The Pill"

Sunglasses

NO SENSE OF HUMOR

THE WOMEN'S MOVEMENT

A PERSON WITH LOW CONSCIOUSNESS LIKE YOURS PROBABLY *WOULD* THINK THAT BRA BURNING IS FUNNY!

WOMEN UNITE!

MEN WHO MADE JOKES ABOUT THE WOMEN'S MOVEMENT

...AND SPEAKING OF WOMEN'S *LIP* — EXCUSE ME, *LIB*, DIDJA HEAR RAQUEL WELCH BURNT HER BRA? ...IT WAS A THREE ALARM FIRE!

...BUT *SERIOUSLY*, FOLKS...

The Message Of The Midi

More Fashion Crimes

INAPPROPRIATE DENIM USE

THE HIGH-WAISTED LOOK

THE HIGH, WASTED LOOK

THE PANTSUIT: JACKALOPE OF THE CLOTHING WORLD?

FRANKENSTEIN STITCHES

THE SEÑOR WENCES SCHOOL OF ORNAMENT

FULL FRONTAL CHEST HAIR

BODY SHIRT: TO ACCENTUATE SLOPING SHOULDERS

THE ANNIE HALL LOOK: DESIGNED TO MAKE WOMEN LOOK SMALL AND VULNERABLE NEXT TO WOODY ALLEN.

"THE BICENTENNIAL LOOK" AND OTHER PROMISCUOUSLY MIXED PATTERNS

1970s MEDIA, ADVERTISING AND FASHION INDUSTRIES UNEASILY MIXED HIPPIE COUNTERCULTURE WITH MIDDLE AMERICAN LUNCH COUNTER CULTURE. THIS PRODUCED MANY STRANGE HYBRIDS TO SATISFY OUR....

Yen for the misbegotten

GARISH SPORT COAT, '50s/'60s + NEHRU JACKET '68 = LEISURE SUIT, 1975

SHORT BACK AND SIDES + THE HIPPIE LOOK = MISTER VELOUR

BROWN FLORSHEIM'S WINGTIPS + DIRTY BARE FEET = EARTH SHOES

ASTAIRE & ROGERS + POST-STONEWALL GAY NIGHTLIFE = DISCO FEVER

craft HELL

FOR A GRIM STRETCH OF THE DECADE IT SEEMED *EVERYONE* WAS "INTO WORKING WITH NATURAL FIBERS," CENTERING THEMSELVES ON THE POTTER'S WHEEL OR SOME OTHER FORM OF HOMESPUN BUSYWORK. IT WAS ALL PART OF THEIR VISION OF A SIMPLE, PASTORAL WORLD WITH A LOT OF TIME ON ITS HANDS, AND FOR A WHILE THE REST OF US HAD TO LIVE IN IT.

Macramé

INEFFECTIVE BELTS

UNSIGHTLY, POSSIBLY UNSANITARY WALL HANGINGS

INTRICATE MACRAMÉ BLOUSE: PERFECT FOR EVENING WEAR OR CASUAL SELF MORTIFICATION

Pottery

PONDEROUS, TOOTH-CHIPPING MUGS (IDEAL FOR BANCHA TEA)

EMBROIDERY:
The Levi's Girlfriend Jacket

EMBROIDERED BY ONE GIRLFRIEND (FOR THEMATIC UNITY)

OR... EMBROIDERED BY SEVERAL NON-POSSESSIVE GIRLFRIENDS (FOR VARIETY)

(STUDS TRANSFORM AN ORDINARY JACKET INTO AN ORDINARY JACKET WITH STUDS.)

Cargo Cult Crafts

The Pop Top Vest

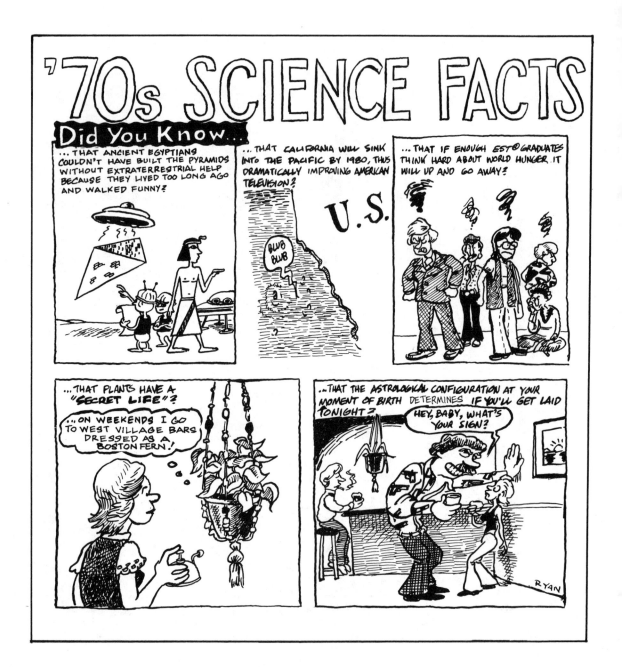

A SEVENTIES CASUALTY